My Behaviour
I Don't Hit

Liz Lennon

W
FRANKLIN WATTS
LONDON•SYDNEY

Sometimes I feel angry.

But I don't hit!

When Mum
won't buy
me sweets,
I feel cross.

But I
don't hit!

Why ... ?

Because hitting hurts and it makes people cry.

My friends left me out at playtime today.

It made me feel sad.

I said to my friends, "I want to play."

But I don't hit!

Sometimes my sister plays with my toys.

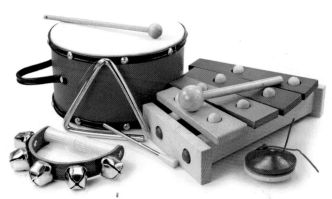

I wish my sister would play with her own toys.

I feel really cross with my sister.

But I don't hit!

Sometimes I
just feel angry.

I don't know why.

There's a knot inside my stomach that makes me feel like hitting out.

When I feel like this, sometimes it's best to be alone.

But other times I tell
someone how I feel.

Either way
I soon
feel better.

And I never, ever hit!

About this book

It is important for young children to learn that hitting is not acceptable, but some children find it hard to express their emotions in other ways. The aim of this book is to give you the opportunity to share and discuss different aspects of behaviour and how it can be managed. Looking at and talking about the pictures is a good starting point.

Why we don't hit The main thing to get across is why we don't hit: because it hurts the person they hit. What would it feel like if someone hit us?

Feeling cross Discuss things that make the child cross such as wanting something they can't have, having to share something of their own or being left out. Why do they feel like this?

What can they do instead? Tell them that their anger or frustration are normal feelings but that they have to express them with words only.

If they hit you If your child hits you, remain calm and make a sad face that shows you are hurt by their behaviour. Tell them: "You hurt me! I'm sad you hit me. Hitting is not okay." Each unacceptable behaviour has to be taken seriously. If you don't act upon it, you'll find it harder to take the control back if your child develops a hitting habit.

If they hit other children Respond quickly and consistently. Never lose your temper. Model empathy by asking the other child if they are all right and apologising on your child's behalf. Remove your child to create distance between the children. Acknowledge your child's feelings, and tell them firmly that hitting is not okay.

First published in 2011
by Franklin Watts

Copyright © Franklin Watts 2011

Franklin Watts
338 Euston Road
London NW1 3BH

Franklin Watts Australia
Level 17/207 Kent Street
Sydney, NSW 2000

All rights reserved.

Printed in China

Series Editor: Sarah Peutrill
Art Director: Jonathan Hair
Series Designer: Paul Cherrill
Picture Researcher: Diana Morris
Consultants: Karina Philip
and Deborah Cox

Franklin Watts is a division of
Hachette Children's Books,
an Hachette UK company.

www.hachette.co.uk

Dewey number: 158.2'5
ISBN: 978 1 4451 0471 3

Picture credits: Fotolia: Godfer 2. Getty Images: Donna Day 12. Istockphoto: MShep2 18. Shutterstock: Blend Images 1, 21; Deepblue-Photographer 16r; Lane V Erickson 7; Gelpi 14, 15; Hartphotography 16l; Crystal Kirk front cover; Monticello 13br; Sergiy N 20; Ami Parikh 17b; Thomas M Perkins 23; Pixel Memoirs 6; Elena Schweitzer 13t, 13cl, 13cr, 13bl; Shebeko 5; John Steel 22; Tikona 17t. Superstock: Image Source 9, 11. Every attempt has been made to clear copyright. Should there be any inadvertent omission please apply to the publisher for rectification.

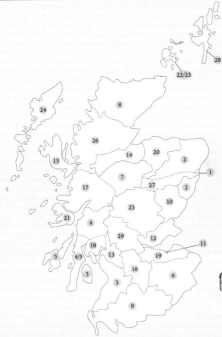

1. Aberdeen
2. Aberdeenshire
3. Arran & Ayrshire
4. Argyll
5. Southern Argyll
6. The Borders
7. The Cairngorms
8. Caithness & Sutherland
9. Dumfries and Galloway
10. Dundee & Angus
11. Edinburgh
12. Fife, Kinross & Clackmannan
13. Glasgow
14. Inverness
15. The Isle of Skye
16. Lanarkshire
17. Lochaber
18. Loch Lomond, Cowal & Bute
19. The Lothians
20. Moray
21. Mull & Iona
22. Orkney
23. Orkney in Wartime
24. The Outer Hebrides
25. Perthshire
26. Ross & Cromarty
27. Royal Deeside
28. Shetland
29. Stirling & The Trossachs

The remaining four books, Caledonia, Distinguished Distilleries, Scotland's Mountains and Scotland's Wildlife feature locations throughout the country so are not included in the above list.

PROPERTY OF SYLVAN GLAMPING
REDBURN IV63 7YJ
RETURN ON DEPARTURE

THE ISLE OF SKYE

NESS PUBLISHING

2   A tantalising sunset glimpse of what awaits – the isles of Skye and Raasay seen from Kyle of Lochalsh.

THE ISLE OF SKYE

Welcome to Skye!

If one was permitted to apply the word 'mystique' to only one part of Scotland, the Inner Hebridean Isle of Skye would almost certainly claim the honour of that description. Its very name in Gaelic, Eilean a'Cheo, Island of Mist, adds to the impression of mystery; the implication that, hidden in those mists, there must be wonders awaiting discovery, secrets to be revealed. Its other name, the Winged Isle, adds another image for the imagination to work on. All but the most hard-hearted or cynical of visitors will find something that affirms those hopes, for Skye is an island that packs a world of contrasts and variety within its shores. Whether seeking extreme scenery, historic diversity or simply the chance to 'chill', Skye will provide.

Skye's geological history has created a land of breathtaking peaks and stunning shapes. The Black Cuillins are undoubtedly the most dramatic mountains in Scotland, so challenging that they attract climbers from all over the world. They are a remnant of Skye's volcanic era, being composed of extremely hard gabbro and basalt rocks. Yet for those with a taste for the weird and wonderful, the landforms of the Trotternish Ridge oblige vividly. In simple terms, what you see here is the result of a number of landslides. This is termed a 'trap' landscape. In volcanic times, lava flows forced their way horizontally between existing layers of sedimentary rocks. Later, the whole landmass tilted to the west, with the eastern edge being uplifted. Here, the great weight of

4

The Skye Bridge, seen here at dawn, crosses the narrows between Kyle of Lochalsh and Kyleakin.   5
Opened in 1995 and now toll-free, it is worth walking onto the bridge for the views it offers.

the basalt lava caused the softer rocks below to give way in a series of huge landslips. The result is the 20-mile line of cliffs along the eastern side of Trotternish, in which the most extreme results of the slippage can be seen at the Storr and the Quiraing.

Skye's human history has also left many marks on the land. There is evidence of habitation going back to Mesolithic times. Just who the first real settlers were, post hunter-gatherer era, is not certain. Opinions vary between Goths from Scandinavia and Goidelic Celts from central Europe. There is much more certainty about the Norsemen who started to arrive around 794 and became the dominant human force in the islands for over 400 years. Many of today's place names, such as those ending in 'aig', testify to their presence. Norse control of the Hebrides came to an end with the Treaty of Perth in 1266 which ceded control of Skye from the Norwegian forces to Scottish rulers. The next few centuries were, broadly speaking, dominated by Clan Donald in the south and Clan MacLeod in the north of the island.

6   The Eilean Ban lighthouse viewed from the Skye Bridge.

Perhaps the most tragic period in Skye's history, and the one that has left much visible evidence (see picture opposite), is the era of the Clearances. These came to Skye later than to some other parts of the Scottish Highlands, such that Skye's population peaked in the early 19th century at a level of approximately 22-23,000. Replacing people with sheep brought this number down drastically: about 7,000 were, in effect, forced to emigrate between 1840 and 1883. After the Clearances ceased, other factors led to continuing decline to a low point of something in the order of 6,000. But in the last 50 years the trend has reversed and today Skye's population is a little over 10,000.

This book works its way around the island from the Skye Bridge down to Sleat in the south, then northwards in a series of excursions into the various peninsulas that make up so much of it. Happy venturing!

The remains of Boreraig, a village deserted during the 19th-century Highland Clearances. 7

8   The Black Cuillin mountain ridge is Skye's most dominant geographic feature, as demonstrated by this picture taken from Portree, 10-12 miles to the north. Pictures like this are quite rare because

normally, by the time of year that the sun is rising in a position that illuminates the north end of the ridge, the snow has gone. This was taken in late March.

10 The village of Kyleakin has been bypassed since the opening of the Skye Bridge but is worth visiting for its various attractions and delightful location.

A closer look at Kyleakin, with the harbour where the ferry used to arrive in the foreground and the 11 remains of Castle Moil beyond. Kyleakin is named after the 13th-century Norse King Hakon.

12 Proceeding now to explore Sleat, the southern part of Skye, we come to Isle Ornsay, once the centre of the fishing industry on Skye.

Left: Isle Ornsay lighthouse guards the Sound of Sleat, beyond which are the mainland mountains. **13**
Right: a couple of miles down the road are the ivy-clad remains of Knock Castle by the village of Teangue.

14 Continuing south and leaving the main road soon after Isle Ornsay, this quiet lochan typifies a prominent aspect of Skye scenery – water dominates so many views. Also ever-present are the distant Cuillins.

Now, from the village of Tokavaig on the west coast of Sleat, the Cuillins are more dominant. **15**
The rocks on the beach seem to mimic the shapes of their grander cousins on the horizon.

16 Taking a closer look: it's at least nine miles from Tokavaig to the dramatic summit of Gars-Bheinn (894m/ 2,932ft), with Ben Meabost on the Elgol peninsula in between. Skye's clear air makes it look nearer.

On the southern edge of Tokavaig, a first glance at a small headland gives the impression of nothing 17 more than a rocky outcrop. But a long lens reveals it's also the remnant of Dunscaith Castle.

18 A couple of miles further on, the picturesque township of Tarskavaig (Norse for 'Cod Bay') spreads itself over this lovely landscape. An idyllic location for those who crave a 'far from the madding crowd' lifestyle

Returning to the east side of Sleat, here are the remains of Armadale Castle. This was the seat of the MacDonalds (Clan Donald), the Lords of the Isles, the medieval rulers of this kingdom.

20 The castle is surrounded by magnificent gardens which today are also the location of the award-winning Museum of the Isles. Here visitors can explore the culture that flourished under the Lords of the Isles.

Ardvasar is just south of Armadale, from where this scene looks across to the mainland district of **21** Knoydart which, ironically, is less accessible than Skye since the Skye Bridge was built.

22 The Aird of Sleat is the southern tip of Skye. From a nearby viewpoint is a panoramic vista across the Sound of Sleat on which the ferry from Mallaig can just be seen, en route to Armadale.

Leaving Sleat behind, we venture north via Broadford (see pp.24-25) and head for the Red Hills and **23** Elgol. With the remains of an ancient cairn in the foreground, Beinn na Caillach is topped in snow.

24 Broadford is the largest in a line of villages around Broadford Bay and is a good base from which to explore Skye. On the east coast of the island, it looks across the Inner Sound towards the Applecros

peninsula on the mainland. Broadford's origins go back to a cattle market held here from the late
1700s. In 1812 the road from Kyleakin to Portree was built by Thomas Telford through the village.

26 A little further along the road from Broadford to Elgol, Loch Cill Chriosd reflects Beinn na Caillach amongst the scant reeds in this early spring scene.

Looking south along the loch, the outline of Bla Bheinn rises in the distance. **27**
Inset: A common sandpiper forages at the edge of the loch.

28 Further along the Elgol road, from the village of Torrin we are treated to the classic view of Bla Bheinn (928m/3045ft) with Loch Slapin in the foreground.

A somewhat more wintry, close-up look at Bla Bheinn, which shows why it is held in high regard by **29** rock climbers and hill walkers. See also p.49 for the view from the other side.

30 Elgol is blessed with one of the most spectacular and perfect views anywhere. The cover picture shows it in spring mode, while here the snow has gone and early summer has arrived.

The translucent waters of Elgol Bay. The rock across the water at the end of the beach has been eroded at the base to form the overhang seen in the right-hand picture on p.34.

32 In contrast to the previous page, winter colours prevail as we zoom in over Loch Scavaig. Sgurr na Stri is on the right.

In close-up, the northern end of the Black Cuillin Ridge shows Am Basteir (934m/3064ft) on the left. **33** Origins of the name are obscure; it might mean 'The executioner'. Sgurr nan Ghillean is on the right.

34 Left: looking in the opposite direction, a fishing boat returns to Elgol, giving a distant glimpse of the islands of Rum and Eigg. Right: severely undercut cliffs on Elgol's boulder beach.

Seals can be seen in many places along Skye's coast. Here a group of common seals take it easy **35** in the June sunshine by Loch Scavaig.

36 Especially if the weather is good, a boat trip across Loch Scavaig to visit Loch Coruisk is a 'must' when visiting Elgol. This view shows the end of Loch Coruisk in the foreground and Loch Scavaig beyond.

Walking around the eastern end of Loch Coruisk opens up the superb vista of the **37** Cuillin ridge enclosing the loch. A path (rough in places) goes right round Coruisk.

38 Sgurr Alasdair, highest of the Cuillin peaks at 992m/3255ft, viewed from Sgurr Dearg, with a challenging stretch of ridge in between. They are largely formed of gabbro, an extremely hard igneous rock.

Darkness falls on the Cuillin ridge but Sgurr na Banachdich is still sunlit. **39**
Two climbers add scale to the scene.

40 Dawn in the Cuillins. The rock from behind which the sun is appearing is the distinctive 'Bhasteir tooth', clearly visible on p.33 to the left of Am Basteir summit.

42 Moving now to the granite-formed Red Cuillins, this dawn view across Loch Ainort shows just why they are so named! Beinn Dearg Mhor is on the left with Glamaig behind and to the right.

Left: as the road curves and climbs round the head of Loch Ainort, this waterfall comes into view. **43**
Right: white-tailed sea eagles have been successfully reintroduced to the Isle of Skye.

44 The high ground north of Loch Ainort gives this impressive long-range view with Ben Tianavaig (413m/1355ft) on the left and, on the right, the Storr (719m/2358ft) about 15 miles away, as the crow flies.

Continuing north up the east side of Skye brings us to Sconser, where the Isle of Raasay rises across **45** the water, with flat-topped Dun Caan forming a most distinctive feature near the centre of the island.

46 An aerial view of Raasay looking north with the village of Clachan in the foreground. The Norse name 'Raasay' means Isle of the Roe or Red Deer. Skye is just visible in the upper left of the picture

Raasay is now on the left as we look south down the Sound of Raasay from Camastianavaig towards **47** The Braes, a settlement on eastern Skye. The Red Cuillins form the horizon on the right.

48 South-west from Sconser is Sligachan, a popular base for hill walkers – it's not hard to see why! Now looking from the north, across Sligachan Burn, the Black Cuillins look both inviting and intimidating

From north of Sligachan and looking through a gap in the Red Cuillins, the awesome northern crags **49** of Bla Bheinn look un-climbable, but some brave souls will have done so.

50 To complete a circuit of the Cuillins we continue west, then south to Glen Brittle. Several paths into the mountains begin here, including the one that passes Eas Mor with its 70m/230ft clear drop.

Looking back, as height is gained, the view into lovely Glen Brittle opens up. Because of the **51** dominance of the Cuillins, the glen does not always get the attention it deserves.

52 For technical difficulty, the Inaccessible Pinnacle (both pictures) takes some beating, but as the official summit of Sgurr Dearg (986m/3235ft) it has to be conquered for the peak to be claimed.

From the Cuillin Ridge a northerly panorama stretches to Skye's more distant parts. **53**
The two flat-topped hills on the horizon are MacLeod's Tables, about 20 miles away (see p.64).

54 Now turning to the south-west, a gap in the clouds illuminates the island of Canna.

Returning to gentler country on the western side of Skye, the inhabitants of Carbost must enjoy the **55** expanse of Loch Harport. This sea loch is typical of many that reach deep into the island.

56 One last look at the Cuillins, as the view along the ridge has to be seen, especially when dramatically lit. This view looks north from Sgurr Alasdair, with Sgurr Dearg towards the left of the picture – the Inaccessible

Pinnacle, catching the light, can be seen protruding above the summit. In total, the Cuillin Ridge comprises 18 individual tops, 14 of which are over 914m/3000ft, 11 of which are classed as Munros.

58 Carbost is best known for Skye's only distillery – Talisker – which produces the internationally famous Talisker single malt Scotch whisky.

Between Sligachan and Carbost, the point of this picture is not (for once!) the snow-capped **59** mountains, but evidence of the old run-rig method of strip farming in the ridges in the foreground.

60 Dun Beag broch stands atop a rocky outcrop near the village of Bracadale on Skye's west coast. As built, this complex, double-walled Iron-Age structure would have been about 10m/33ft taller.

High points in this vicinity are ideal for catching Skye sunsets. The promontories of Loch Bracadale **61**
and Loch Varka stand out in this light.

62 St Mary's Church, Dunvegan probably has roots that go back to the Columban era of early Christian missionaries. These ruins are pre-Reformation, this church being replaced in the 1830s.

Just up the hill from St Mary's, all is not quite what it might seem, as this standing stone is not an **63** ancient monument but was erected by the Dunvegan community in 2000 to mark the 21st century.

64 The northern part of Skye comprises three peninsulas, the westernmost of which is Duirinish, location of Healabhal Mor and Healabhal Bheag, otherwise known as MacLeod's Tables, referred to earlier.

Dunvegan Castle has been continuously owned by the MacLeod family for very nearly eight centuries. **65**
Architecturally, it is a structure of high importance, containing work of at least ten building periods.

66 Dunvegan Castle Gardens were originally laid out in the 18th century. This is the walled garden.

What a cute little lamb! Sheep are a common sight on the roads and fields of Skye.

68 Travelling north-west through the wilds of Duirinish reveals occasional settlements such as Glendale and Milovaig, both of which overlook Loch Pooltiel, seen here from Meanish Pier.

final two or three miles bring us to the most westerly extremity of Skye, Neist Point. The lighthouse, **69** built in 1909 and fully automated in 1990, is 19m/62ft high. Its light is equal to 480,000 candles.

70 Head north from Dunvegan, drive to the end of the road then walk for about 30 minutes and you'll arrive at the beautiful Coral Sands. The sand is not in fact coral but comprises desiccated algae and

eaweed as well as broken shells. But whatever it's made of, this is a perfect spot on the right day,
ith views to other parts of Skye and the Outer Hebrides on the horizon.

72 A foretaste of what's to come on the western side of the Trotternish peninsula, this is Uig (the name means 'bay') with the village of Idrigill on the far side. Places to see in Uig include the Fairy Glen

(see p.94), and Uig waterfall. Uig is the ferry port for the Outer Hebrides (on the horizon), with routes to the islands of North Uist and Harris. The ferry *Hebrides* prepares to sail.

74 The Waternish peninsula lies between those of Duirinish and Trotternish and is seen here beyond the headlands on the right. See also the back cover picture.

Skye's main town is Portree, seen here from the south. The final leg of this tour is to Trotternish, Skye's north-eastern peninsula and location of a classic example of a 'trap' landscape (see Introduction).

76 Portree's picture-perfect harbour. Portree means 'King's Haven', a reference to the visit of James V in 1540, when the king was on a mission to subdue rebellious elements in the Hebrides.

Loch Portree on a summer evening. It was in Portree that Bonnie Prince Charlie bade farewell for the last time to Flora MacDonald, who had famously aided him after the Battle of Culloden in 1746.

78 One of the most spectacular features on the Trotternish Ridge is the Storr, which is encountered about five miles north of Portree. It is seen here across Loch Fada on a still winter morning.

A succession of landslips on the eastern edge of the ridge has resulted in a proliferation of basalt **79** pinnacles, the best known being the 50m/165ft Old Man of Storr, on the right of the picture.

80 The view back from the base of The Old Man shows more improbable shapes. A few figures can be seen on the paths, giving an idea of the scale of the scene.

The base of The Old Man of Storr is narrower than the rest, which enables pictures like this, **81** th the overhang on the right framing the view to the north, with yet another pinnacle standing tall.

82 Left: continuing north, this waterfall drains Loch Mealt into the sea and is close to the Kilt Rock (right). This cliff is so named because of the vertical strata's resemblance to the pleats of a kilt.

The village of Staffin is a mile or two north of Kilt Rock. Inset: Columba 1400 in Staffin, named to **83** honour the 1400th anniversary of St Columba's mission to Scotland.

84 From the slopes of the Quiraing, this is the view south along the Trotternish Ridge with the Storr in the far distance. Walking the whole length of the ridge is a distance of 36.5km/22.75 miles.

Turning round and looking at the Quiraing itself, the slip-zone is clear to see. The largest **85** mass-movement slide in Britain, extending in total over 2km in width and slowly heading for the sea.

86 The Quiraing towers above the villages of Staffin and Brogaig. From the jaws of the crags we see a vertigo-inducing drop down to Staffin Bay.

Left: not too surprisingly, this pinnacle is known as the Needle. Right: from high inside the **87** Quiraing, another vertical drop before the next part of the shattered, crumbling ridge.

88 The magnificent view from the south: for many, the Quiraing is the ultimate demonstration on Skye of the 'trap' landscape. In this panorama from Loch Mealt, the scale of the landslip which has

occurred can be appreciated. It's not hard to visualise how the angular block on the right would once have joined the main part of the massif on the left. 'Quiraing' is Norse for 'folded ridge'.

90 It is well worth the hour's walk from the car park visible in p.84's picture to climb the hill above the Quiraing so as to be able to look down into this amazing landscape, centrepiece of which is the Tabl

een here tucked into the upper folds of the slip zone. To get a fix on where we are, refer back to
.88 and look for the jagged rocks just below the highest point of the hill: the Table is there.

92 Duntulm Castle, at the northern tip of Skye, began as an Iron-Age broch, then a Viking stronghold before being rebuilt as a castle, firstly by the MacLeods and later by the MacDonalds.

The Museum of Island Life is situated between Duntulm and Uig. It preserves a township of thatched **93** cottages, each one depicting the conditions prevailing on the island at the close of the nineteenth century.

94 Inland from Uig is the curious landscape-in-miniature known as the Fairy Glen. The rocky tower (known as Castle Ewen) is a natural feature, but the same can't be said for the stones at bottom left

Journey's end: a view of Uig that looks across the bay to where the picture on pp.72-73 was taken **95** from. The gentler, western slope of the Trotternish ridge (seen on p.84) rises beyond.

Published 2014 by Ness Publishing, 47 Academy Street, Elgin, Moray, IV30 1LR. Reprinted 2015 (twice) and 2016.
Phone 01343 549663 www.nesspublishing.co.uk
(First published 2010 as *The Isle of Skye: a pictorial souvenir* and reprinted 2012 & 2013)

All photographs © Colin and Eithne Nutt except pp.2-3, 40-41 & 56-57 © Alan Gordon/Highland Light; p.27 (inset)
© Sue M. Cleave; p.39 © David Paterson; p.43 (right) © Laurie Campbell; p.46 © Scotavia Images; p.48 © Ian Evans/
Mountain Images; p.66 © Dunvegan Castle; back cover © Pat Myhill

Text © Colin Nutt

ISBN 978-1-906549-38-1

Front cover: The Cuillins from Elgol; p.1: fishing boat near Kyleakin; p.4: otter sculpture at Kyleakin;
this page: Brewery at Uig; back cover: Waternish Peninsula

For a list of websites and phone numbers please turn over >

Websites and phone numbers (where available) of featured places in alphabetical order:

Armadale Castle/Clan Donald Centre: www.clandonald.com (T) 01471 844305 or 01471 844227
Broadford: www.isleofskye.com/tour/broadford
Caledonian MacBrayne ferries: www.calmac.co.uk (T) 0800 066 5000
Columba 1400: www.columba1400.com (T) 01478 611400
Duirinish: www.glendaleskye.com
Dun Beag broch: www.historic-scotland.gov.uk (T) 01667 460232
Duntulm Castle: www.ambaile.org.uk
Dunvegan Castle: www.dunvegancastle.com (T): 01470 521206
Elgol: www.isleofskye.com
Isle of Raasay: www.raasay.com
Isle of Skye Brewery: www.skyebrewery.co.uk (T) 01470 542477
Isle of Skye: www.isleofskye.com
Museum of Island Life: www.skyemuseum.co.uk (T) 01470 552206
Portree: www.isleofskye.com
Sleat: www.visitsleat.org
Talisker Distillery: www.discovering-distilleries.com/talisker (T) 01478 614308
The Cuillins: www.munromagic.com
The Quiraing: www.scottishgeology.com
The Storr: walking.visitscotland.com
Trotternish: website.lineone.net/~trotternish
Uig: www.uig-isleofskye.com
Waternish: www.visit-waternish.co.uk